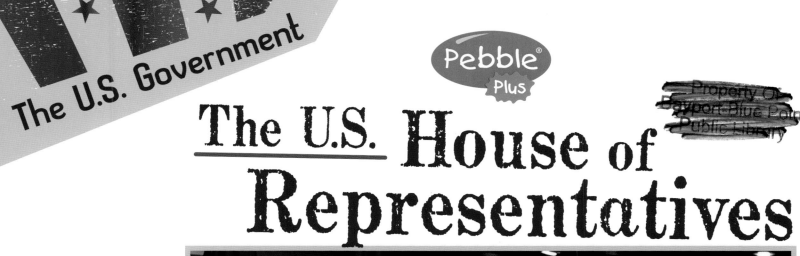

Pebble Plus

The U.S. House of Representatives

by Mari Schuh

Consulting Editor: Gail Saunders-Smith, PhD

Consultant: Steven S. Smith, Kate M. Gregg Distinguished Professor
of Social Sciences and Professor of Political Science
Director, Weidenbaum Center on the Economy, Government, and Public Policy
Washington University, St. Louis, Missouri

CAPSTONE PRESS
a capstone imprint

Pebble Plus is published by Capstone Press,
1710 Roe Crest Drive, North Mankato, Minnesota 56003.
www.capstonepub.com

Books published by Capstone Press are manufactured with paper containing at least 10 percent post-consumer waste.

Library of Congress Cataloging-in-Publication Data
Schuh, Mari C., 1975–
  The U.S. House of Representatives / by Mari Schuh.
    p. cm.—(Pebble plus. The U.S. government)
  Includes bibliographical references and index.
  Summary: "Simple text and full-color photographs provide a brief introduction to the U.S. House of Representatives"—Provided by publisher.
  ISBN 978-1-4296-7565-9 (library binding)
  1. United States. Congress. House—Juvenile literature. 2. Legislators—United States--Juvenile literature. I. Title. II. Title: US House of Representatives. III. Title: United States House of Representatives.
  JK1319.S36 2012
  328.73'072—dc23   2011021661

Editorial Credits

Erika L. Shores, editor; Ashlee Suker, designer, Kathy McColley, production specialist

Photo Credits

Bloomberg via Getty Images/Brendan Hoffman, 1, 13
Corbis/Ted Soqui, 15
Getty Images/Alex Wong, cover; Congressional Quarterly/Scott J. Ferrell, 17; Roll Call/Tom Williams, 5
newscom/LA Opinion/Aurelia Ventura, 11
Official White House photo by Pete Souza, 9, 19, 21
The Washington Post via Getty Images/Bill O'Leary, 7

Artistic Effects

Shutterstock: Christophe BOISSON

The author dedicates this book to her brother-in-law Duane Quam, Jr., a member of the Minnesota House of Representatives, and to Chris Krizek, Executive Director of the Wheaton Franciscan Healthcare-All Saints Foundation in Racine, Wisconsin.

Note to Parents and Teachers

The U.S. Government series supports national history standards related to understanding the importance of and basic principles of American democracy. This book describes and illustrates the U.S. House of Representatives. The images support early readers in understanding the text. The repetition of words and phrases helps early readers learn new words. This book also introduces early readers to subject-specific vocabulary words, which are defined in the Glossary section. Early readers may need assistance to read some words and to use the Table of Contents, Glossary, Read More, Internet Sites, and Index sections of the book.

Printed in the United States of America in North Mankato, Minnesota.
102011   006405CGS12

Table of Contents

Making Laws

The U.S. House of Representatives

works in Washington, D.C.,

to make laws. Laws start as bills.

Representatives work together to

make new laws for the country.

Three Branches

The U.S. government has
three branches. Congress is
the legislative branch. The House
of Representatives and the Senate
are the two parts of Congress.

IN GOD WE TRUST

The executive branch puts laws into effect and makes sure people follow them. The president leads the executive branch. The judicial branch explains the laws.

Becoming a Representative

Representatives are elected to work

for the people in their home state.

States with many people have

more representatives.

Representatives serve two-year terms.

Representatives must be age 25 or older and live in the state where they're elected. They need to be U.S. citizens for at least seven years before being elected.

Representatives at Work

Representatives meet with
the citizens of their state.
Representatives find out
what new laws people want.

In Washington, D.C.,

representatives work on committees

to study bills and laws.

Representatives vote on bills,

go to events, and meet with leaders.

MR. ENGEL
NEW YORK

MR. STUPAK
MICHIGAN

MS. ESHOO
CALIFORNIA

MR. RUSH
ILLINOIS

MR. GONZALEZ
TEXAS

MS. BALDWIN
WISCONSIN

MS. CASTOR
FLORIDA

The Speaker of the House
leads the U.S. House.
The speaker often meets
with the president to talk
about bills.

Speaker of the House John Boehner (left), Vice President Joe Biden (middle), and President Barack Obama (right) meet in the Oval Office.

The same bill needs to be passed

in the House and the Senate.

If the president signs the bill,

it becomes a new law.

Glossary

bill—a written plan for a new law; the U.S. House of Representatives and the U.S. Senate write bills

committee—a small group of people chosen to discuss things and make decisions for a larger group

elect—to choose someone by voting

executive branch—the part of the U.S. government that makes sure people follow the laws

judicial branch—the part of the U.S. government that explains the laws; the courts make up the judicial branch

law—a rule made by the government that must be obeyed

Senate—a part of the U.S. government that makes laws, along with the U.S. House of Representatives

term—a set period of time elected leaders serve in office

Read More

Gorman, Jacqueline Laks. *Member of Congress.* Know Your Government. Pleasantville, N.Y.: Weekly Reader, 2009.

Jakubiak, David J. *What Does a Congressional Representative Do?* How Our Government Works. New York: PowerKids Press, 2010.

Taylor-Butler, Christine. *The Congress of the United States.* A True Book. New York: Children's Press, 2008.

Internet Sites

FactHound offers a safe, fun way to find Internet sites related to this book. All of the sites on FactHound have been researched by our staff.

Here's all you do:

Visit *www.facthound.com*

Type in this code: 9781429675659

Check out projects, games and lots more at
www.capstonekids.com

23

Index

Word Count: 210
Grade: 1
Early-Intervention Level: 20